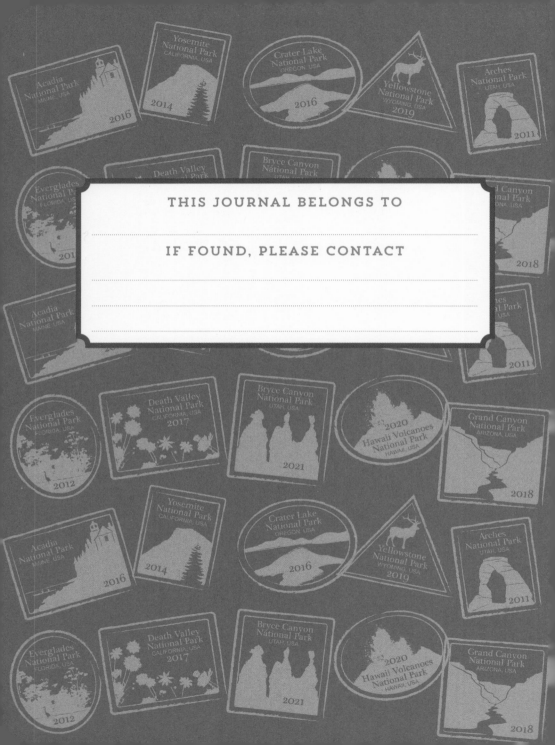

THIS JOURNAL BELONGS TO

....

IF FOUND, PLEASE CONTACT

....

....

....

USA
NATIONAL
PARKS
JOURNAL
═══and═══
PASSPORT STAMP BOOK

Peter Pauper Press, Inc.
RYE BROOK, NEW YORK

PETER PAUPER PRESS
Fine Books and Gifts Since 1928

Our Company

In 1928, at the age of twenty-two, Peter Beilenson began printing books on a small press in the basement of his parents' home in Larchmont, New York. Peter—and later, his wife, Edna—sought to create fine books that sold at "prices even a pauper could afford."

Today, still family owned and operated, Peter Pauper Press continues to honor our founders' legacy—and our customers' expectations—of beauty, quality, and value.

Designed by David Cole Wheeler
Images used under license from Shutterstock.com

Copyright © 2023
Peter Pauper Press, Inc.
3 International Drive
Rye Brook, NY 10573 USA

ISBN 978-1-4413-4014-6
Printed in China

7 6 5 4 3

USA NATIONAL PARKS MAP
AND OTHER NPS PASSPORT SITES

MAP NOT TO SCALE

ME
NH
MA
VT
RI
CT
NY
NJ
DE
MD
DC
PA
WV
VA
NC
SC
OH
GA
MI
IN
KY
TN
AL
IL
WI
MS
IA
MO
AR
LA
MN
ND
SD
NE
KS
OK
TX
MT
WY
CO
NM
ID
UT
AZ
WA
NV
OR
CA
AK
HI
VI
PR
AS

TABLE OF CONTENTS

INTRODUCTION

The United States hosts more than 400 beautiful parks, historic sites, and memorials across its vast and varied expanse. Each national park contains treasures of nature and culture, just waiting to be explored. Let this journal entice you to discover the vast beauty of the nation.

This volume contains all 63 designated U.S. national parks, plus a selection of 37 of the most well-known and well-traveled NPS sites of each state and territory, from monuments and historic sites to national seashores and scenic trails. Use the extra pages in the back to include stamps from other parks you visit.

Treat each spread as an adventure log. When you arrive at each park, flip to its corresponding page and jot down your memories and experiences. Each spread also contains a space to collect each park's passport stamp(s), with extra pages in the back for further travels. In time, this book will become a keepsake chronicling your adventures through all 50 states and then some.

ACADIA NATIONAL PARK, ME

Date visited: .... Weather: ☀ ⛅ ☁ ⛅ ☁ ⛈ ☁ ☁ ☁

Traveling companions: ....

Where we stayed: ....

What we did: ....

....

....

Sights seen: ....

....

....

Wildlife seen: ....

....

....

Favorite moments: ....

....

....

....

....

....

....

....

....

....

PASSPORT STAMP(S)

Favorite attractions: ....
....
....

Visit again? .... Park rating: ☆ ☆ ☆ ☆ ☆

Things to remember for next time: ....
....
....

NOTES

....
....
....
....
....
....
....

ARCHES NATIONAL PARK, UT

Date visited: .... Weather: ☀ ⛅ ☁ ⛅ 🌧 ⛈ ☁ 🌨 🌨

Traveling companions: ....

Where we stayed: ....

What we did: ....

....

....

....

Sights seen: ....

....

....

....

Wildlife seen: ....

....

....

....

Favorite moments: ....

....

....

....

....

....

....

....

....

....

PASSPORT STAMP(S)

Favorite attractions:

Visit again?   Park rating: ☆ ☆ ☆ ☆ ☆

Things to remember for next time:

NOTES

BADLANDS NATIONAL PARK, SD

Date visited: .... Weather: ☀ ⛅ ☁ ⛅ 🌧 ⛈ ☁ 🌨 🌨

Traveling companions: ....

Where we stayed: ....

What we did: ....

....

....

Sights seen: ....

....

....

Wildlife seen: ....

....

....

Favorite moments: ....

....

....

....

....

....

....

....

....

PASSPORT STAMP(S)

Favorite attractions:

Visit again?   Park rating: ☆ ☆ ☆ ☆ ☆

Things to remember for next time:

NOTES

BIG BEND NATIONAL PARK, TX

Date visited: .... Weather: ☀ 🌦 ☁ 🌤 ☁ ⛈ ☁ 🌨 🌨

Traveling companions: ....

Where we stayed: ....

What we did: ....

....

....

....

Sights seen: ....

....

....

....

Wildlife seen: ....

....

....

....

Favorite moments: ....

....

....

....

....

....

....

....

....

PASSPORT STAMP(S)

Favorite attractions:

Visit again?   Park rating: ☆ ☆ ☆ ☆ ☆

Things to remember for next time:

NOTES

BISCAYNE NATIONAL PARK, FL

Date visited: .... Weather: ☀️ ⛅🌧️ ☁️ ⛅ 🌧️ ⛈️ ☁️ 🌨️ 🌨️

Traveling companions: ....

Where we stayed: ....

What we did: ....

....

....

Sights seen: ....

....

....

Wildlife seen: ....

....

....

Favorite moments: ....

....

....

....

....

....

....

....

....

PASSPORT STAMP(S)

Favorite attractions:

Visit again?   Park rating: ☆ ☆ ☆ ☆ ☆

Things to remember for next time:

NOTES

BLACK CANYON OF THE GUNNISON NATIONAL PARK, CO

Date visited: _____ Weather: ☀ ⛅ ☁ 🌤 🌦 ⛈ 🌧 🌨 🌨

Traveling companions: _____

Where we stayed: _____

What we did: _____

_____

_____

Sights seen: _____

_____

_____

Wildlife seen: _____

_____

_____

Favorite moments: _____

_____

_____

_____

_____

_____

_____

_____

_____

PASSPORT STAMP(S)

Favorite attractions:

Visit again?   Park rating: ☆ ☆ ☆ ☆ ☆

Things to remember for next time:

NOTES

BRYCE CANYON NATIONAL PARK, UT

Date visited: .... Weather: ☀ ⛅ ☁ ⛅ ☁ ⛈ ☁ ☁ ☁

Traveling companions: ....

Where we stayed: ....

What we did: ....

....

....

Sights seen: ....

....

....

Wildlife seen: ....

....

....

Favorite moments: ....

....

....

....

....

....

....

....

....

PASSPORT STAMP(S)

Favorite attractions:

Visit again?   Park rating: ☆ ☆ ☆ ☆ ☆

Things to remember for next time:

NOTES

CANYONLANDS NATIONAL PARK, UT

Date visited: .... Weather: ☀ ⛅ ☁ ⛅ ☁ ⛈ ☁ ❄ 🌨

Traveling companions: ....

Where we stayed: ....

What we did: ....

....

....

Sights seen: ....

....

....

Wildlife seen: ....

....

....

Favorite moments: ....

....

....

....

....

....

....

....

....

PASSPORT STAMP(S)

Favorite attractions:

Visit again?   Park rating: ☆ ☆ ☆ ☆ ☆

Things to remember for next time:

NOTES

CAPITOL REEF NATIONAL PARK, UT

Date visited: .... Weather: ☀ ⛅ ☁ ⛅ 🌧 ⛈ ☁ 🌨 🌨

Traveling companions: ....

Where we stayed: ....

What we did: ....

....

....

Sights seen: ....

....

....

Wildlife seen: ....

....

....

Favorite moments: ....

....

....

....

....

....

....

....

....

PASSPORT STAMP(S)

Favorite attractions:

Visit again?   Park rating: ☆ ☆ ☆ ☆ ☆

Things to remember for next time:

NOTES

CARLSBAD CAVERNS NATIONAL PARK, NM

Date visited: ....   Weather: ☀ ⛅ ☁ ⛅ 🌧 ⛈ ☁ 🌨 🌨

Traveling companions: ....

Where we stayed: ....

What we did: ....

....

....

Sights seen: ....

....

....

Wildlife seen: ....

....

....

Favorite moments: ....

....

....

....

....

....

....

....

....

....

PASSPORT STAMP(S)

Favorite attractions:

Visit again?   Park rating: ☆ ☆ ☆ ☆ ☆

Things to remember for next time:

NOTES

CHANNEL ISLANDS NATIONAL PARK, CA

Date visited: .... Weather:

Traveling companions: ....

Where we stayed: ....

What we did: ....

....

....

Sights seen: ....

....

....

Wildlife seen: ....

....

....

Favorite moments: ....

....

....

....

....

....

....

....

....

....

PASSPORT STAMP(S)

Favorite attractions: ....

....

....

Visit again? .... Park rating: ☆ ☆ ☆ ☆ ☆

Things to remember for next time: ....

....

NOTES

....

....

....

....

....

....

CONGAREE NATIONAL PARK, SC

Date visited: .... Weather: ☀ ⛅ ☁ ⛅ 🌧 ⛈ ☁ ❄ 🌨

Traveling companions: ....

Where we stayed: ....

What we did: ....

....

....

....

Sights seen: ....

....

....

Wildlife seen: ....

....

....

Favorite moments: ....

....

....

....

....

....

....

....

....

....

....

PASSPORT STAMP(S)

Favorite attractions:

Visit again?   Park rating: ☆ ☆ ☆ ☆ ☆

Things to remember for next time:

NOTES

CRATER LAKE NATIONAL PARK, OR

Date visited: .... Weather: ☀ ⛅ ☁ ⛅ ☁ ⛈ ☁ ❄ ❄

Traveling companions: ....

Where we stayed: ....

What we did: ....

....

....

Sights seen: ....

....

....

Wildlife seen: ....

....

....

Favorite moments: ....

....

....

....

....

....

....

....

....

....

PASSPORT STAMP(S)

Favorite attractions:

Visit again?   Park rating: ☆ ☆ ☆ ☆ ☆

Things to remember for next time:

NOTES

CUYAHOGA VALLEY NATIONAL PARK, OH

Date visited: .... Weather:

Traveling companions: ....

Where we stayed: ....

What we did: ....

....

....

Sights seen: ....

....

....

Wildlife seen: ....

....

....

Favorite moments: ....

....

....

....

....

....

....

....

PASSPORT STAMP(S)

Favorite attractions:

Visit again?   Park rating: ☆ ☆ ☆ ☆ ☆

Things to remember for next time:

NOTES

DEATH VALLEY NATIONAL PARK, CA/NV

Date visited: .... Weather: ☀ ⛅ ☁ ⛅ 🌧 ⛈ ☁ 🌨 🌨

Traveling companions: ....

Where we stayed: ....

What we did: ....

....

....

Sights seen: ....

....

'

Wildlife seen: ....

....

....

Favorite moments: ....

....

....

....

....

....

....

....

....

....

PASSPORT STAMP(S)

Favorite attractions:

Visit again? .... Park rating: ☆ ☆ ☆ ☆ ☆

Things to remember for next time:

NOTES

DENALI NATIONAL PARK AND PRESERVE, AK

Date visited: .... Weather: ☀ ☁ ☁ ☁ ☁ ⚡ ☁ ❄ ❄

Traveling companions: ....

Where we stayed: ....

What we did: ....

....

....

....

Sights seen: ....

....

....

....

Wildlife seen: ....

....

....

....

Favorite moments: ....

....

....

....

....

....

....

....

....

....

PASSPORT STAMP(S)

Favorite attractions:

Visit again?   Park rating: ☆ ☆ ☆ ☆ ☆

Things to remember for next time:

NOTES

DRY TORTUGAS NATIONAL PARK, FL

Date visited: .... Weather: ☀️ 🌦️ ☁️ ⛅ 🌧️ ⛈️ 🌥️ 🌨️ 🌨️

Traveling companions: ....

Where we stayed: ....

What we did: ....

....

....

....

Sights seen: ....

....

....

Wildlife seen: ....

....

....

Favorite moments: ....

....

....

....

....

....

....

....

....

....

....

PASSPORT STAMP(S)

Favorite attractions: ....
....
....

Visit again? .... Park rating: ☆ ☆ ☆ ☆ ☆

Things to remember for next time: ....
....
....

NOTES

....
....
....
....
....
....

EVERGLADES NATIONAL PARK, FL

Date visited: _____   Weather: ☀ ⛅ ☁ ⛅ ☁ ⛈ ☁ ☁ ☁

Traveling companions: _____

Where we stayed: _____

What we did: _____

_____

_____

Sights seen: _____

_____

_____

Wildlife seen: _____

_____

_____

Favorite moments: _____

_____

_____

_____

_____

_____

_____

_____

_____

PASSPORT STAMP(S)

Favorite attractions:

Visit again?   Park rating: ☆ ☆ ☆ ☆ ☆

Things to remember for next time:

NOTES

GATES OF THE ARCTIC NATIONAL PARK AND PRESERVE, AK

Date visited: .... Weather: ☀ ⛅ ☁ ⛅ 🌧 ⛈ ☁ 🌨 🌨

Traveling companions: ....

Where we stayed: ....

What we did: ....

....

....

Sights seen: ....

....

....

Wildlife seen: ....

....

....

Favorite moments: ....

....

....

....

....

....

....

....

....

PASSPORT STAMP(S)

Favorite attractions:

Visit again?   Park rating: ☆ ☆ ☆ ☆ ☆

Things to remember for next time:

NOTES

GATEWAY ARCH NATIONAL PARK, MO/IL

Date visited: .... Weather: ☀ ⛅ ☁ 🌤 🌧 ⛈ ☁ 🌨 🌨

Traveling companions: ....

Where we stayed: ....

What we did: ....

....

....

Sights seen: ....

....

....

Wildlife seen: ....

....

....

Favorite moments: ....

....

....

....

....

....

....

....

....

....

PASSPORT STAMP(S)

Favorite attractions:

Visit again?   Park rating: ☆ ☆ ☆ ☆ ☆

Things to remember for next time:

NOTES

GLACIER BAY NATIONAL PARK AND PRESERVE, AK

Date visited: _____ Weather: ☀️ 🌦️ ☁️ ⛅ 🌧️ ⛈️ 🌥️ 🌨️ 🌨️

Traveling companions: _____

Where we stayed: _____

What we did: _____

_____

_____

Sights seen: _____

_____

_____

Wildlife seen: _____

_____

_____

Favorite moments: _____

_____

_____

_____

_____

_____

_____

_____

_____

PASSPORT STAMP(S)

Favorite attractions:

Visit again?   Park rating: ☆ ☆ ☆ ☆ ☆

Things to remember for next time:

NOTES

GLACIER NATIONAL PARK, MT

Date visited: .... Weather: ☀ 🌦 ☁ ⛅ 🌧 ⛈ 🌥 🌨 🌨

Traveling companions: ....

Where we stayed: ....

What we did: ....

....

....

Sights seen: ....

....

....

Wildlife seen: ....

....

....

Favorite moments: ....

....

....

....

....

....

....

....

....

PASSPORT STAMP(S)

Favorite attractions:

Visit again? .... Park rating: ☆ ☆ ☆ ☆ ☆

Things to remember for next time:

NOTES

GRAND CANYON NATIONAL PARK, AZ

Date visited: .... Weather: ☀ ⛅ ☁ 🌤 🌧 ⛈ ☁ 🌨 🌨

Traveling companions: ....

Where we stayed: ....

What we did: ....

....

....

....

Sights seen: ....

....

....

Wildlife seen: ....

....

....

Favorite moments: ....

....

....

....

....

....

....

....

....

....

....

PASSPORT STAMP(S)

Favorite attractions:

Visit again?   Park rating: ☆ ☆ ☆ ☆ ☆

Things to remember for next time:

NOTES

GRAND TETON NATIONAL PARK, WY

Date visited: .... Weather: ☀ 🌦 ☁ 🌤 🌧 ⛈ ☁ 🌨 🌨

Traveling companions: ....

Where we stayed: ....

What we did: ....

....

....

Sights seen: ....

....

....

Wildlife seen: ....

....

....

Favorite moments: ....

....

....

....

....

....

....

....

....

PASSPORT STAMP(S)

Favorite attractions:

Visit again?   Park rating: ☆ ☆ ☆ ☆ ☆

Things to remember for next time:

NOTES

GREAT BASIN NATIONAL PARK, NV

Date visited: .... Weather: ☀ ⛅ ☁ ⛅ 🌧 ⛈ 🌥 🌨 🌨

Traveling companions: ....

Where we stayed: ....

What we did: ....

....

....

Sights seen: ....

....

....

Wildlife seen: ....

....

....

Favorite moments: ....

....

....

....

....

....

....

....

....

....

....

PASSPORT STAMP(S)

Favorite attractions: ....
....
....

Visit again? .... Park rating: ☆ ☆ ☆ ☆ ☆

Things to remember for next time: ....
....
....

NOTES

....
....
....
....
....
....

GREAT SAND DUNES NATIONAL PARK AND PRESERVE, CO

Date visited:............... Weather: ☀ 🌦 ☁ 🌤 🌧 ⛈ ☁ 🌨 🌨

Traveling companions:...

Where we stayed:..

What we did:...

....

....

Sights seen:...

....

....

Wildlife seen:...

....

....

Favorite moments:...

....

....

....

....

....

....

....

....

PASSPORT STAMP(S)

Favorite attractions:

Visit again?   Park rating: ☆ ☆ ☆ ☆ ☆

Things to remember for next time:

NOTES

GREAT SMOKY MOUNTAINS NATIONAL PARK, NC/TN

Date visited: .... Weather: ☀ ⛅ ☁ ⛅ 🌧 ⛈ ☁ 🌨 🌨

Traveling companions: ....

Where we stayed: ....

What we did: ....

....

....

Sights seen: ....

....

....

Wildlife seen: ....

....

....

Favorite moments: ....

....

....

....

....

....

....

....

....

PASSPORT STAMP(S)

Favorite attractions:

Visit again?   Park rating: ☆ ☆ ☆ ☆ ☆

Things to remember for next time:

NOTES

GUADALUPE MOUNTAINS NATIONAL PARK, TX

Date visited: .... Weather: ☀ ⛅ ☁ ⛅ ☁ ⛈ ☁ ☁ ☁

Traveling companions: ....

Where we stayed: ....

What we did: ....

....

....

Sights seen: ....

....

....

Wildlife seen: ....

....

....

Favorite moments: ....

....

....

....

....

....

....

....

....

....

....

PASSPORT STAMP(S)

Favorite attractions:

Visit again? .... Park rating: ☆ ☆ ☆ ☆ ☆

Things to remember for next time:

NOTES

HALEAKALĀ NATIONAL PARK, HI

Date visited: .... Weather: ☀ 🌦 ☁ 🌤 🌧 ⛈ ☁ 🌨 🌨

Traveling companions: ....

Where we stayed: ....

What we did: ....

....

....

Sights seen: ....

....

....

Wildlife seen: ....

....

....

Favorite moments: ....

....

....

....

....

....

....

....

....

PASSPORT STAMP(S)

Favorite attractions:

Visit again?   Park rating: ☆ ☆ ☆ ☆ ☆

Things to remember for next time:

NOTES

HAWAI'I VOLCANOES NATIONAL PARK, HI

Date visited: .... Weather: ☀ ⛅ ☁ 🌤 ☁ ⛈ ☁ 🌨 🌨

Traveling companions: ....

Where we stayed: ....

What we did: ....

....

....

Sights seen: ....

....

....

Wildlife seen: ....

....

....

Favorite moments: ....

....

....

....

....

....

....

....

....

PASSPORT STAMP(S)

Favorite attractions:

Visit again?   Park rating: ☆ ☆ ☆ ☆ ☆

Things to remember for next time:

NOTES

HOT SPRINGS NATIONAL PARK, AR

Date visited: .... Weather: ☀ 🌦 ☁ ⛅ 🌧 ⛈ ☁ 🌨 🌨

Traveling companions: ....

Where we stayed: ....

What we did: ....

....

....

Sights seen: ....

....

....

Wildlife seen: ....

....

....

Favorite moments: ....

....

....

....

....

....

....

....

....

PASSPORT STAMP(S)

Favorite attractions:

Visit again?   Park rating: ☆ ☆ ☆ ☆ ☆

Things to remember for next time:

NOTES

INDIANA DUNES NATIONAL PARK, IN

Date visited: .... Weather: ☀ ⛅ ☁ 🌤 🌦 ⛈ ☁ 🌨 🌨

Traveling companions: ....

Where we stayed: ....

What we did: ....

Sights seen: ....

Wildlife seen: ....

Favorite moments: ....

PASSPORT STAMP(S)

Favorite attractions:

Visit again?   Park rating: ☆ ☆ ☆ ☆ ☆

Things to remember for next time:

NOTES

ISLE ROYALE NATIONAL PARK, MI

Date visited: _____ Weather: ☀ ⛅ ☁ 🌤 🌧 ⛈ 🌥 🌨 🌨

Traveling companions: _____

Where we stayed: _____

What we did: _____

_____

_____

_____

Sights seen: _____

_____

_____

Wildlife seen: _____

_____

_____

Favorite moments: _____

_____

_____

_____

_____

_____

_____

_____

_____

_____

PASSPORT STAMP(S)

Favorite attractions:

Visit again?   Park rating: ☆ ☆ ☆ ☆ ☆

Things to remember for next time:

NOTES

JOSHUA TREE NATIONAL PARK, CA

Date visited: .... Weather: ☀ ⛅ ☁ ⛅ 🌧 ⛈ ☁ ❄ 🌨

Traveling companions: ....

Where we stayed: ....

What we did: ....

....

....

Sights seen: ....

....

....

Wildlife seen: ....

....

....

Favorite moments: ....

....

....

....

....

....

....

....

PASSPORT STAMP(S)

Favorite attractions:

Visit again?   Park rating: ☆ ☆ ☆ ☆ ☆

Things to remember for next time:

NOTES

KATMAI NATIONAL PARK AND PRESERVE, AK

Date visited: .... Weather: ☀ ⛅ ☁ ⛅ 🌧 ⛈ ☁ 🌨 🌨

Traveling companions: ....

Where we stayed: ....

What we did: ....

....

....

....

Sights seen: ....

....

....

....

Wildlife seen: ....

....

....

....

Favorite moments: ....

....

....

....

....

....

....

....

....

....

PASSPORT STAMP(S)

Favorite attractions:

Visit again?   Park rating: ☆ ☆ ☆ ☆ ☆

Things to remember for next time:

NOTES

KENAI FJORDS NATIONAL PARK, AK

Date visited: .... Weather: ☀ ⛅ ☁ ⛅ 🌧 ⛈ ☁ 🌨 🌨

Traveling companions: ....

Where we stayed: ....

What we did: ....

Sights seen: ....

Wildlife seen: ....

Favorite moments: ....

PASSPORT STAMP(S)

Favorite attractions:

Visit again?   Park rating: ☆ ☆ ☆ ☆ ☆

Things to remember for next time:

NOTES

KINGS CANYON NATIONAL PARK, CA

Date visited: _____ Weather: ☀ ⛅ ☁ ⛅ ☁ ⛈ ☁ ❄ 🌨

Traveling companions: _____

Where we stayed: _____

What we did: _____

_____

_____

Sights seen: _____

_____

_____

Wildlife seen: _____

_____

_____

Favorite moments: _____

_____

_____

_____

_____

_____

_____

_____

_____

PASSPORT STAMP(S)

Favorite attractions:

Visit again?   Park rating: ☆ ☆ ☆ ☆ ☆

Things to remember for next time:

NOTES

KOBUK VALLEY NATIONAL PARK, AK

Date visited: .... Weather: ☀ 🌦 ☁ 🌤 🌧 ⛈ ☁ 🌨 🌨

Traveling companions: ....

Where we stayed: ....

What we did: ....

....

....

Sights seen: ....

....

....

Wildlife seen: ....

....

....

Favorite moments: ....

....

....

....

....

....

....

....

PASSPORT STAMP(S)

Favorite attractions:

Visit again?   Park rating: ☆ ☆ ☆ ☆ ☆

Things to remember for next time:

NOTES

LAKE CLARK NATIONAL PARK AND PRESERVE, AK

Date visited: .... Weather: ☀ ⛅ ☁ ⛅ 🌧 ⛈ ☁ 🌨 🌨

Traveling companions: ....

Where we stayed: ....

What we did: ....

....

....

Sights seen: ....

....

....

Wildlife seen: ....

....

....

Favorite moments: ....

....

....

....

....

....

....

....

....

....

PASSPORT STAMP(S)

Favorite attractions:

Visit again?   Park rating: ☆ ☆ ☆ ☆ ☆

Things to remember for next time:

NOTES

LASSEN VOLCANIC NATIONAL PARK, CA

Date visited:............................ Weather: ☀ ⛅ ☁ ⛅ 🌧 ⛈ ☁ 🌨 🌨

Traveling companions:..

Where we stayed:..

What we did:..

....

....

....

Sights seen:...

....

....

Wildlife seen:...

....

....

Favorite moments:..

....

....

....

....

....

....

....

....

....

PASSPORT STAMP(S)

Favorite attractions:

Visit again?   Park rating: ☆ ☆ ☆ ☆ ☆

Things to remember for next time:

NOTES

MAMMOTH CAVE NATIONAL PARK, KY

Date visited: .... Weather: ☀ 🌤 ☁ 🌤 🌧 ⛈ ☁ 🌨 🌨

Traveling companions: ....

Where we stayed: ....

What we did: ....

....

....

Sights seen: ....

....

....

Wildlife seen: ....

....

....

Favorite moments: ....

....

....

....

....

....

....

....

....

....

PASSPORT STAMP(S)

Favorite attractions:

Visit again?   Park rating: ☆ ☆ ☆ ☆ ☆

Things to remember for next time:

NOTES

MESA VERDE NATIONAL PARK, CO

Date visited: .... Weather: ☀ ⛅ ☁ ⛅ 🌧 ⛈ ☁ 🌨 🌨

Traveling companions: ....

Where we stayed: ....

What we did: ....

....

....

Sights seen: ....

....

....

Wildlife seen: ....

....

....

Favorite moments: ....

....

....

....

....

....

....

....

....

PASSPORT STAMP(S)

Favorite attractions:

Visit again?   Park rating: ☆ ☆ ☆ ☆ ☆

Things to remember for next time:

NOTES

MOUNT RAINIER NATIONAL PARK, WA

Date visited: .... Weather: ☀ ⛅ ☁ ⛅ 🌧 ⛈ ☁ 🌨 🌨

Traveling companions: ....

Where we stayed: ....

What we did: ....

....

....

....

Sights seen: ....

....

....

Wildlife seen: ....

....

....

Favorite moments: ....

....

....

....

....

....

....

....

....

PASSPORT STAMP(S)

Favorite attractions:

Visit again?   Park rating: ☆ ☆ ☆ ☆ ☆

Things to remember for next time:

NOTES

NATIONAL PARK OF
AMERICAN SAMOA, AS

Date visited: .... Weather: ☀ ⛅ ☁ ⛅ ☁ ⛈ ☁ ☁ ☁

Traveling companions: ....

Where we stayed: ....

What we did: ....

....

....

....

Sights seen: ....

....

....

....

Wildlife seen: ....

....

....

....

Favorite moments: ....

....

....

....

....

....

....

....

....

....

PASSPORT STAMP(S)

Favorite attractions:

Visit again?   Park rating: ☆ ☆ ☆ ☆ ☆

Things to remember for next time:

NOTES

NEW RIVER GORGE NATIONAL PARK AND PRESERVE, WV

Date visited: .... Weather: ☀ ⛅ ☁ 🌤 🌧 ⛈ 🌨 🌨

Traveling companions: ....

Where we stayed: ....

What we did: ....

....

....

Sights seen: ....

....

....

Wildlife seen: ....

....

....

Favorite moments: ....

....

....

....

....

....

....

....

....

....

PASSPORT STAMP(S)

Favorite attractions:

Visit again?   Park rating: ☆ ☆ ☆ ☆ ☆

Things to remember for next time:

NOTES

NORTH CASCADES NATIONAL PARK, WA

Date visited: .... Weather: ☀ ⛈ ☁ ⛅ ☁ ⛈ ☁ ☃ ☃

Traveling companions: ....

Where we stayed: ....

What we did: ....

....

....

Sights seen: ....

....

....

Wildlife seen: ....

....

....

Favorite moments: ....

....

....

....

....

....

....

....

PASSPORT STAMP(S)

Favorite attractions:

Visit again?... Park rating: ☆ ☆ ☆ ☆ ☆

Things to remember for next time:

NOTES

OLYMPIC NATIONAL PARK, WA

Date visited: .... Weather: ☀ ⛅ ☁ ⛅ 🌧 ⛈ ☁ ❄ 🌨

Traveling companions: ....

Where we stayed: ....

What we did: ....

....

....

Sights seen: ....

....

....

Wildlife seen: ....

....

....

Favorite moments: ....

....

....

....

....

....

....

....

....

PASSPORT STAMP(S)

Favorite attractions:

Visit again?   Park rating: ☆ ☆ ☆ ☆ ☆

Things to remember for next time:

NOTES

PETRIFIED FOREST NATIONAL PARK, AZ

Date visited: .... Weather: ☀ ⛅ ☁ ⛅ 🌧 ⛈ 🌦 🌨 🌨

Traveling companions: ....

Where we stayed: ....

What we did: ....

....

....

Sights seen: ....

....

....

Wildlife seen: ....

....

....

Favorite moments: ....

....

....

....

....

....

....

....

....

....

PASSPORT STAMP(S)

Favorite attractions:

Visit again? _____ Park rating: ☆ ☆ ☆ ☆ ☆

Things to remember for next time:

NOTES

PINNACLES NATIONAL PARK, CA

Date visited: .... Weather: ☀ ⛅ ☁ ⛅ 🌧 ⛈ ☁ 🌨 🌨

Traveling companions: ....

Where we stayed: ....

What we did: ....

....

....

Sights seen: ....

....

....

Wildlife seen: ....

....

....

Favorite moments: ....

....

....

....

....

....

....

....

....

....

PASSPORT STAMP(S)

Favorite attractions:

Visit again?   Park rating: ☆ ☆ ☆ ☆ ☆

Things to remember for next time:

NOTES

REDWOOD NATIONAL PARK, CA

Date visited: .... Weather: ☀ ⛅ ☁ ⛅ 🌧 ⛈ ☁ 🌨 🌨

Traveling companions: ....

Where we stayed: ....

What we did: ....

....

....

Sights seen: ....

....

....

Wildlife seen: ....

....

....

Favorite moments: ....

....

....

....

....

....

....

....

....

....

PASSPORT STAMP(S)

Favorite attractions:

Visit again? _____ Park rating: ☆ ☆ ☆ ☆ ☆

Things to remember for next time:

NOTES

ROCKY MOUNTAIN NATIONAL PARK, CO

Date visited: .... Weather:

Traveling companions: ....

Where we stayed: ....

What we did: ....

....

....

....

Sights seen: ....

....

....

Wildlife seen: ....

....

....

Favorite moments: ....

....

....

....

....

....

....

....

....

....

PASSPORT STAMP(S)

Favorite attractions:

Visit again?   Park rating: ☆ ☆ ☆ ☆ ☆

Things to remember for next time:

NOTES

SAGUARO NATIONAL PARK, AZ

Date visited: .... Weather: ☀ ⛅ ☁ ⛅ ☁ ⛈ ☁ ☁ ☁

Traveling companions: ....

Where we stayed: ....

What we did: ....

....

....

Sights seen: ....

....

....

Wildlife seen: ....

....

....

Favorite moments: ....

....

....

....

....

....

....

....

....

PASSPORT STAMP(S)

Favorite attractions:

Visit again?   Park rating: ☆ ☆ ☆ ☆ ☆

Things to remember for next time:

NOTES

SEQUOIA NATIONAL PARK, CA

Date visited: .... Weather: ☀ ⛅ ☁ ⛅ ☁ ⛈ ☁ ❄ ☃

Traveling companions: ....

Where we stayed: ....

What we did: ....

....

....

Sights seen: ....

....

....

Wildlife seen: ....

....

....

Favorite moments: ....

....

....

....

....

....

....

....

....

....

PASSPORT STAMP(S)

Favorite attractions:

Visit again?   Park rating: ☆ ☆ ☆ ☆ ☆

Things to remember for next time:

NOTES

SHENANDOAH NATIONAL PARK, VA

Date visited: .... Weather: ☀️ 🌦️ ☁️ 🌦️ 🌧️ ⛈️ ☁️ 🌨️ 🌨️

Traveling companions: ....

Where we stayed: ....

What we did: ....

....

....

Sights seen: ....

....

....

Wildlife seen: ....

....

....

Favorite moments: ....

....

....

....

....

....

....

....

....

PASSPORT STAMP(S)

Favorite attractions:

Visit again?   Park rating: ☆ ☆ ☆ ☆ ☆

Things to remember for next time:

NOTES

THEODORE ROOSEVELT
NATIONAL PARK, ND

Date visited: .... Weather: ☀ 🌦 ☁ 🌤 🌧 ⛈ ☁ 🌨 🌨

Traveling companions: ....

Where we stayed: ....

What we did: ....

....

....

....

Sights seen: ....

....

....

Wildlife seen: ....

....

....

Favorite moments: ....

....

....

....

....

....

....

....

....

....

PASSPORT STAMP(S)

Favorite attractions:

Visit again? .... Park rating: ☆ ☆ ☆ ☆ ☆

Things to remember for next time:

NOTES

VIRGIN ISANDS NATIONAL PARK, VI

Date visited: .... Weather: ☀ ⛅ ☁ 🌦 🌧 ⛈ ☁ 🌨 🌨

Traveling companions: ....

Where we stayed: ....

What we did: ....

....

....

Sights seen: ....

....

....

Wildlife seen: ....

....

....

Favorite moments: ....

....

....

....

....

....

....

....

PASSPORT STAMP(S)

Favorite attractions:

Visit again?   Park rating: ☆ ☆ ☆ ☆ ☆

Things to remember for next time:

NOTES

VOYAGEURS NATIONAL PARK, MN

Date visited: .... Weather: ☀ ⛅ ☁ ⛅ 🌧 ⛈ ☁ 🌨 🌨

Traveling companions: ....

Where we stayed: ....

What we did: ....

....

....

Sights seen: ....

....

....

Wildlife seen: ....

....

....

Favorite moments: ....

....

....

....

....

....

....

....

....

....

PASSPORT STAMP(S)

Favorite attractions:

Visit again?   Park rating: ☆ ☆ ☆ ☆ ☆

Things to remember for next time:

NOTES

WHITE SANDS NATIONAL PARK, NM

Date visited: _____ Weather: ☀ ⛅ ☁ ⛅ 🌧 ⛈ ☁ 🌨 🌨

Traveling companions: ....

Where we stayed: ....

What we did: ....

....

....

Sights seen: ....

....

....

Wildlife seen: ....

....

....

Favorite moments: ....

....

....

....

....

....

....

....

....

....

....

PASSPORT STAMP(S)

Favorite attractions:

Visit again?   Park rating: ☆ ☆ ☆ ☆ ☆

Things to remember for next time:

NOTES

WIND CAVE NATIONAL PARK, SD

Date visited: .... Weather: ☀ ⛅ ☁ ⛅ 🌧 ⛈ ☁ 🌨 🌨

Traveling companions: ....

Where we stayed: ....

What we did: ....

....

....

....

Sights seen: ....

....

....

Wildlife seen: ....

....

....

Favorite moments: ....

....

....

....

....

....

....

....

....

PASSPORT STAMP(S)

Favorite attractions:

Visit again?   Park rating: ☆ ☆ ☆ ☆ ☆

Things to remember for next time:

NOTES

WRANGELL–ST. ELIAS NATIONAL PARK AND PRESERVE, AK

Date visited: _____ Weather: ☀ ⛅ ☁ ⛅ 🌧 ⛈ ☁ 🌨 🌨

Traveling companions: _____

Where we stayed: _____

What we did: _____

_____

_____

Sights seen: _____

_____

_____

Wildlife seen: _____

_____

_____

Favorite moments: _____

_____

_____

_____

_____

_____

_____

_____

_____

_____

PASSPORT STAMP(S)

Favorite attractions:

Visit again?   Park rating: ☆ ☆ ☆ ☆ ☆

Things to remember for next time:

NOTES

YELLOWSTONE
NATIONAL PARK, ID/MT/WY

Date visited: .... Weather: ☀ ⛅ ☁ 🌤 🌧 ⛈ 🌨 ☁❄ 🌨

Traveling companions: ....

Where we stayed: ....

What we did: ....

....

....

Sights seen: ....

....

....

Wildlife seen: ....

....

....

Favorite moments: ....

....

....

....

....

....

....

....

....

PASSPORT STAMP(S)

Favorite attractions:

Visit again?   Park rating: ☆ ☆ ☆ ☆ ☆

Things to remember for next time:

NOTES

YOSEMITE NATIONAL PARK, CA

Date visited: .... Weather: ☀ ⛈ ☁ ⛅ 🌧 ⛈ ☁ 🌨 🌨

Traveling companions: ....

Where we stayed: ....

What we did: ....

....

....

Sights seen: ....

....

....

Wildlife seen: ....

....

....

Favorite moments: ....

....

....

....

....

....

....

....

....

PASSPORT STAMP(S)

Favorite attractions:

Visit again? Park rating: ☆ ☆ ☆ ☆ ☆

Things to remember for next time:

NOTES

ZION NATIONAL PARK, UT

Date visited: .... Weather: ☀ ⛅ ☁ 🌤 🌧 ⛈ ☁ 🌨 🌨

Traveling companions: ....

Where we stayed: ....

What we did: ....

....

....

Sights seen: ....

....

....

Wildlife seen: ....

....

....

Favorite moments: ....

....

....

....

....

....

....

....

....

PASSPORT STAMP(S)

Favorite attractions:

Visit again?   Park rating: ☆ ☆ ☆ ☆ ☆

Things to remember for next time:

NOTES

APOSTLE ISLANDS
NATIONAL LAKESHORE, WI

Date visited: .... Weather: ☀ ⛅ ☁ 🌤 🌦 ⛈ ☁ 🌨 🌨

Traveling companions: ....

Where we stayed: ....

What we did: ....

....

....

Sights seen: ....

....

....

Wildlife seen: ....

....

....

Favorite moments: ....

....

....

....

....

....

....

....

PASSPORT STAMP(S)

Favorite attractions:

Visit again? .... Park rating: ☆ ☆ ☆ ☆ ☆

Things to remember for next time:

NOTES

APPALACHIAN NATIONAL SCENIC TRAIL

Date visited: .... Weather: ☀ ⛅ ☁ ⛅ 🌧 ⛈ ☁ 🌨 🌨

Traveling companions: ....

Where we stayed: ....

What we did: ....

....

....

Sights seen: ....

....

....

Wildlife seen: ....

....

....

Favorite moments: ....

....

....

....

....

....

....

....

....

PASSPORT STAMP(S)

Favorite attractions:

Visit again?   Park rating: ☆ ☆ ☆ ☆ ☆

Things to remember for next time:

NOTES

ASSATEAGUE ISLAND NATIONAL SEASHORE, MD/VA

Date visited: .... Weather: ☀ ⛅ ☁ ⛅ 🌧 ⛈ ☁ 🌨 🌨

Traveling companions: ....

Where we stayed: ....

What we did: ....

....

....

....

Sights seen: ....

....

....

Wildlife seen: ....

....

....

Favorite moments: ....

....

....

....

....

....

....

....

....

PASSPORT STAMP(S)

Favorite attractions:

Visit again?   Park rating: ☆ ☆ ☆ ☆ ☆

Things to remember for next time:

NOTES

BLUE RIDGE PARKWAY, NC/VA

Date visited: .... Weather: ☀ ⛅ ☁ ⛅ 🌧 ⛈ ☁ ❄ 🌨

Traveling companions: ....

Where we stayed: ....

What we did: ....

....

....

....

Sights seen: ....

....

....

Wildlife seen: ....

....

....

Favorite moments: ....

....

....

....

....

....

....

....

PASSPORT STAMP(S)

Favorite attractions:

Visit again?   Park rating: ☆ ☆ ☆ ☆ ☆

Things to remember for next time:

NOTES

CAPE COD NATIONAL SEASHORE, MA

Date visited: .... Weather: ☀ ⛅ ☁ ⛅ 🌧 ⛈ ☁ 🌨 🌨

Traveling companions: ....

Where we stayed: ....

What we did: ....

....

....

Sights seen: ....

....

....

Wildlife seen: ....

....

....

Favorite moments: ....

....

....

....

....

....

....

....

....

....

PASSPORT STAMP(S)

Favorite attractions:

Visit again?   Park rating: ☆ ☆ ☆ ☆ ☆

Things to remember for next time:

NOTES

CHESAPEAKE & OHIO CANAL
NATIONAL HISTORICAL PARK, DC/MD/WV

Date visited: .... Weather: ☀ 🌦 ☁ 🌤 🌧 ⛈ ☁ 🌨 🌨

Traveling companions: ....

Where we stayed: ....

What we did: ....
....
....
....

Sights seen: ....
....
....
....

Wildlife seen: ....
....
....
....

Favorite moments: ....
....
....
....
....
....
....
....
....
....

PASSPORT STAMP(S)

Favorite attractions:

Visit again?   Park rating: ☆ ☆ ☆ ☆ ☆

Things to remember for next time:

NOTES

CRATERS OF THE MOON NATIONAL MONUMENT AND PRESERVE, ID

Date visited: .... Weather: ☀ ⛅ ☁ ⛅ ☁ ⛈ ☁ ☁ ☁

Traveling companions: ....

Where we stayed: ....

What we did: ....

....

....

Sights seen: ....

....

....

Wildlife seen: ....

....

....

Favorite moments: ....

....

....

....

....

....

....

....

....

PASSPORT STAMP(S)

Favorite attractions:

Visit again?   Park rating: ☆ ☆ ☆ ☆ ☆

Things to remember for next time:

NOTES

CUMBERLAND GAP
NATIONAL HISTORICAL PARK, KY/TN/VA

Date visited: .... Weather: ☀ ⛅ ☁ ⛅ 🌧 ⛈ 🌨 ☁ 🌨

Traveling companions: ....

Where we stayed: ....

What we did: ....

....

....

Sights seen: ....

....

....

Wildlife seen: ....

....

....

Favorite moments: ....

....

....

....

....

....

....

....

....

PASSPORT STAMP(S)

Favorite attractions:

Visit again?   Park rating: ☆ ☆ ☆ ☆ ☆

Things to remember for next time:

NOTES

DELAWARE WATER GAP
NATIONAL RECREATION AREA, NJ/PA

Date visited: .... Weather: ☀ ⛅ ☁ 🌥 🌧 ⛈ ☁ 🌨 🌨

Traveling companions: ....

Where we stayed: ....

What we did: ....

....

....

....

Sights seen: ....

....

....

Wildlife seen: ....

....

....

Favorite moments: ....

....

....

....

....

....

....

....

....

....

PASSPORT STAMP(S)

Favorite attractions:

Visit again?   Park rating: ☆ ☆ ☆ ☆ ☆

Things to remember for next time:

NOTES

EFFIGY MOUNDS
NATIONAL MONUMENT, IA

Date visited: .... Weather:

Traveling companions: ....

Where we stayed: ....

What we did: ....

....

....

Sights seen: ....

....

....

Wildlife seen: ....

....

....

Favorite moments: ....

....

....

....

....

....

....

....

....

PASSPORT STAMP(S)

Favorite attractions:

Visit again?   Park rating: ☆ ☆ ☆ ☆ ☆

Things to remember for next time:

NOTES

FIRST STATE
NATIONAL HISTORICAL PARK, DE/PA

Date visited: .... Weather: ☀ ⛅ ☁ 🌤 🌧 ⛈ ☁ 🌨 🌨

Traveling companions: ....

Where we stayed: ....

What we did: ....

....

....

Sights seen: ....

....

....

Wildlife seen: ....

....

....

Favorite moments: ....

....

....

....

....

....

....

....

....

PASSPORT STAMP(S)

Favorite attractions:

Visit again? .... Park rating: ☆ ☆ ☆ ☆ ☆

Things to remember for next time:

NOTES

FORT SUMTER AND FORT MOULTRIE NATIONAL HISTORICAL PARK, SC

Date visited: .... Weather:

Traveling companions: ....

Where we stayed: ....

What we did: ....

....

....

....

Sights seen: ....

....

....

....

Wildlife seen: ....

....

....

Favorite moments: ....

....

....

....

....

....

....

....

....

....

PASSPORT STAMP(S)

Favorite attractions:

Visit again? .... Park rating: ☆ ☆ ☆ ☆ ☆

Things to remember for next time:

NOTES

GATEWAY NATIONAL RECREATION AREA, NJ/NY

Date visited: .... Weather: ☀ ⛅ ☁ 🌤 🌧 ⛈ ☁ 🌨 🌨

Traveling companions: ....

Where we stayed: ....

What we did: ....

....

....

Sights seen: ....

....

....

Wildlife seen: ....

....

....

Favorite moments: ....

....

....

....

....

....

....

....

....

....

PASSPORT STAMP(S)

Favorite attractions:

Visit again?   Park rating: ☆ ☆ ☆ ☆ ☆

Things to remember for next time:

NOTES

GLEN CANYON
NATIONAL RECREATION AREA, UT/AZ

Date visited: .... Weather: ☀ 🌦 ☁ 🌤 🌧 ⛈ ☁ 🌨 🌨

Traveling companions: ....

Where we stayed: ....

What we did: ....

....

....

Sights seen: ....

....

....

Wildlife seen: ....

....

....

Favorite moments: ....

....

....

....

....

....

....

....

....

....

PASSPORT STAMP(S)

Favorite attractions:

Visit again?   Park rating: ☆ ☆ ☆ ☆ ☆

Things to remember for next time:

NOTES

GULF ISLANDS
NATIONAL SEASHORE, FL/MS

Date visited: .... Weather: ☀ ⛅ ☁ ⛅ ☁ ⛈ ☁ ☁ ☁

Traveling companions: ....

Where we stayed: ....

What we did: ....

....

....

....

Sights seen: ....

....

....

....

Wildlife seen: ....

....

....

....

Favorite moments: ....

....

....

....

....

....

....

....

....

PASSPORT STAMP(S)

Favorite attractions:

Visit again?   Park rating: ☆ ☆ ☆ ☆ ☆

Things to remember for next time:

NOTES

INDEPENDENCE
NATIONAL HISTORICAL PARK, PA

Date visited: .... Weather: ☀ ⛅ ☁ ⛅ ☁ ⛈ ☁ ☁ ☁

Traveling companions: ....

Where we stayed: ....

What we did: ....

....

....

....

Sights seen: ....

....

....

Wildlife seen: ....

....

....

Favorite moments: ....

....

....

....

....

....

....

....

....

PASSPORT STAMP(S)

Favorite attractions:

Visit again?   Park rating: ☆ ☆ ☆ ☆ ☆

Things to remember for next time:

NOTES

JEAN LAFITTE NATIONAL HISTORICAL PARK AND PRESERVE, LA

Date visited: _____ Weather: ☀ ⛅ ☁ ⛅ 🌧 ⛈ ☁ 🌨 🌨

Traveling companions: _____

Where we stayed: _____

What we did: _____

_____

_____

Sights seen: _____

_____

_____

Wildlife seen: _____

_____

_____

Favorite moments: _____

_____

_____

_____

_____

_____

_____

_____

PASSPORT STAMP(S)

Favorite attractions:

Visit again?   Park rating: ☆ ☆ ☆ ☆ ☆

Things to remember for next time:

NOTES

LINCOLN HOME
NATIONAL HISTORIC SITE, IL

Date visited: .... Weather: ☀ ⛅ ☁ ⛅ 🌧 ⛈ ☁ 🌨 🌨

Traveling companions: ....

Where we stayed: ....

What we did: ....

....

....

....

Sights seen: ....

....

....

Wildlife seen: ....

....

....

Favorite moments: ....

....

....

....

....

....

....

....

....

PASSPORT STAMP(S)

Favorite attractions:

Visit again?   Park rating: ☆ ☆ ☆ ☆ ☆

Things to remember for next time:

NOTES

LINCOLN MEMORIAL, DC

Date visited: .... Weather: ☀ ⛅ ☁ ⛅ 🌦 ⛈ ☁ 🌨 🌨

Traveling companions: ....

Where we stayed: ....

What we did: ....

....

....

Sights seen: ....

....

....

Wildlife seen: ....

....

....

Favorite moments: ....

....

....

....

....

....

....

....

....

PASSPORT STAMP(S)

Favorite attractions:

Visit again?   Park rating: ☆ ☆ ☆ ☆ ☆

Things to remember for next time:

NOTES

MARSH-BILLINGS-ROCKEFELLER NATIONAL HISTORICAL PARK, VT

Date visited: .... Weather:

Traveling companions: ....

Where we stayed: ....

What we did: ....

....

....

Sights seen: ....

....

....

Wildlife seen: ....

....

....

Favorite moments: ....

....

....

....

....

....

....

....

....

....

....

PASSPORT STAMP(S)

Favorite attractions:

Visit again?   Park rating: ☆ ☆ ☆ ☆ ☆

Things to remember for next time:

NOTES

MARTIN LUTHER KING, JR. MEMORIAL, DC

Date visited: .... Weather: ☀ ⛅ ☁ 🌤 🌧 ⛈ ☁ 🌨 🌨

Traveling companions: ....

Where we stayed: ....

What we did: ....

....

....

Sights seen: ....

....

....

Wildlife seen: ....

....

....

Favorite moments: ....

....

....

....

....

....

....

....

PASSPORT STAMP(S)

Favorite attractions:

Visit again?   Park rating: ☆ ☆ ☆ ☆ ☆

Things to remember for next time:

NOTES

NATCHEZ TRACE PARKWAY, AL/MS/TN

Date visited: .... Weather: ☀ ⛅ ☁ ⛅ 🌧 ⛈ ☁ 🌨 🌨

Traveling companions: ....

Where we stayed: ....

What we did: ....

....

....

Sights seen: ....

....

....

Wildlife seen: ....

....

....

Favorite moments: ....

....

....

....

....

....

....

....

....

PASSPORT STAMP(S)

Favorite attractions:

Visit again?   Park rating: ☆ ☆ ☆ ☆ ☆

Things to remember for next time:

NOTES

NEZ PERCE
NATIONAL HISTORICAL PARK, ID/MT/OR/WA

Date visited: .... Weather: ☀ 🌦 ☁ ⛅ 🌧 ⛈ ☁ 🌨 🌨

Traveling companions: ....

Where we stayed: ....

What we did: ....

....

....

Sights seen: ....

....

....

Wildlife seen: ....

....

....

Favorite moments: ....

....

....

....

....

....

....

....

....

PASSPORT STAMP(S)

Favorite attractions:

Visit again?   Park rating: ☆ ☆ ☆ ☆ ☆

Things to remember for next time:

NOTES

OCMULGEE MOUNDS
NATIONAL HISTORICAL PARK, GA

Date visited: .... Weather: ☀ ⛅ ☁ 🌤 ☁ ⛈ ☁ ❄ 🌨

Traveling companions: ....

Where we stayed: ....

What we did: ....

....

....

Sights seen: ....

....

....

Wildlife seen: ....

....

....

Favorite moments: ....

....

....

....

....

....

....

....

PASSPORT STAMP(S)

Favorite attractions:

Visit again?   Park rating: ☆ ☆ ☆ ☆ ☆

Things to remember for next time:

NOTES

OZARK
NATIONAL SCENIC RIVERWAYS, MO

Date visited: .... Weather: ☀ ⛈ ☁ ⛅ 🌧 ⚡ ☁ 🌨 🌨

Traveling companions: ....

Where we stayed: ....

What we did: ....

....

....

Sights seen: ....

....

....

Wildlife seen: ....

....

....

Favorite moments: ....

....

....

....

....

....

....

....

....

PASSPORT STAMP(S)

Favorite attractions:

Visit again?   Park rating: ☆ ☆ ☆ ☆ ☆

Things to remember for next time:

NOTES

PICTURED ROCKS
NATIONAL LAKESHORE, MI

Date visited: .... Weather: ☀ 🌧 ☁ ⛅ 🌦 ⛈ ☁ 🌨 🌨

Traveling companions: ....

Where we stayed: ....

What we did: ....

....

....

....

Sights seen: ....

....

....

Wildlife seen: ....

....

....

Favorite moments: ....

....

....

....

....

....

....

....

....

PASSPORT STAMP(S)

Favorite attractions:

Visit again?   Park rating: ☆ ☆ ☆ ☆ ☆

Things to remember for next time:

NOTES

ROGER WILLIAMS
NATIONAL MEMORIAL, RI

Date visited: .... Weather:

Traveling companions: ....

Where we stayed: ....

What we did: ....

....

....

Sights seen: ....

....

....

Wildlife seen: ....

....

....

Favorite moments: ....

....

....

....

....

....

....

....

PASSPORT STAMP(S)

Favorite attractions:

Visit again?   Park rating: ☆ ☆ ☆ ☆ ☆

Things to remember for next time:

NOTES

SAINT CROIX
NATIONAL SCENIC RIVERWAY, MN/WI

Date visited: .... Weather: ☀ ⛅ ☁ ⛅ ☁ ⛈ ☁ ❄ 🌨

Traveling companions: ....

Where we stayed: ....

What we did: ....

....

....

Sights seen: ....

....

....

Wildlife seen: ....

....

....

Favorite moments: ....

....

....

....

....

....

....

....

....

....

PASSPORT STAMP(S)

Favorite attractions:

Visit again?   Park rating: ☆ ☆ ☆ ☆ ☆

Things to remember for next time:

NOTES

SAINT-GAUDENS
NATIONAL HISTORICAL PARK, NH

Date visited: .... Weather: ☀ ⛅ ☁ ⛅ ☁ ⛈ ☁ ❄ 🌨

Traveling companions: ....

Where we stayed: ....

What we did: ....

....

....

Sights seen: ....

....

....

Wildlife seen: ....

....

....

Favorite moments: ....

....

....

....

....

....

....

....

....

PASSPORT STAMP(S)

Favorite attractions:

Visit again?   Park rating: ☆ ☆ ☆ ☆ ☆

Things to remember for next time:

NOTES

SAN FRANCISCO MARITIME
NATIONAL HISTORICAL PARK, CA

Date visited: .... Weather: ☀ ⛅ ☁ ⛅ 🌧 ⛈ ☁ 🌨 🌨

Traveling companions: ....

Where we stayed: ....

What we did: ....

....

....

Sights seen: ....

....

....

Wildlife seen: ....

....

....

Favorite moments: ....

....

....

....

....

....

....

....

....

PASSPORT STAMP(S)

Favorite attractions:

Visit again?   Park rating: ☆ ☆ ☆ ☆ ☆

Things to remember for next time:

NOTES

SAN JUAN NATIONAL HISTORIC SITE, PR

Date visited: .... Weather: ☀ ⛅ ☁ ⛅ 🌧 ⛈ ☁ 🌨 🌨

Traveling companions: ....

Where we stayed: ....

What we did: ....

....

....

Sights seen: ....

....

....

Wildlife seen: ....

....

....

Favorite moments: ....

....

....

....

....

....

....

....

PASSPORT STAMP(S)

Favorite attractions:

Visit again?   Park rating: ☆ ☆ ☆ ☆ ☆

Things to remember for next time:

NOTES

SCOTTS BLUFF NATIONAL MONUMENT, NE

Date visited: .... Weather: ☀ ⛅ ☁ 🌤 🌧 ⛈ ☁ 🌨 🌨

Traveling companions: ....

Where we stayed: ....

What we did: ....

....

....

Sights seen: ....

....

....

Wildlife seen: ....

....

....

Favorite moments: ....

....

....

....

....

....

....

....

....

PASSPORT STAMP(S)

Favorite attractions:

Visit again?   Park rating: ☆ ☆ ☆ ☆ ☆

Things to remember for next time:

NOTES

SLEEPING BEAR DUNES
NATIONAL LAKESHORE, MI

Date visited: .... Weather: ☀ ⛅ ☁ ⛅ 🌧 ⛈ ☁ 🌨 🌨

Traveling companions: ....

Where we stayed: ....

What we did: ....

....

....

Sights seen: ....

....

....

Wildlife seen: ....

....

....

Favorite moments: ....

....

....

....

....

....

....

....

....

PASSPORT STAMP(S)

Favorite attractions:

Visit again?   Park rating: ☆ ☆ ☆ ☆ ☆

Things to remember for next time:

NOTES

STATUE OF LIBERTY
NATIONAL MONUMENT, NJ/NY

Date visited: .... Weather: ☀ ⛅ ☁ ⛅ ☁ ⛈ ☁ ❄ 🌨

Traveling companions: ....

Where we stayed: ....

What we did: ....

....

....

Sights seen: ....

....

....

Wildlife seen: ....

....

....

Favorite moments: ....

....

....

....

....

....

....

....

....

....

PASSPORT STAMP(S)

Favorite attractions:

Visit again?   Park rating: ☆ ☆ ☆ ☆ ☆

Things to remember for next time:

NOTES

TALLGRASS PRAIRIE NATIONAL PRESERVE, KS

Date visited: .... Weather:

Traveling companions: ....

Where we stayed: ....

What we did: ....

....

....

Sights seen: ....

....

....

Wildlife seen: ....

....

....

Favorite moments: ....

....

....

....

....

....

....

....

....

PASSPORT STAMP(S)

Favorite attractions:

Visit again?   Park rating: ☆ ☆ ☆ ☆ ☆

Things to remember for next time:

NOTES

WASHITA BATTLEFIELD
NATIONAL HISTORIC SITE, OK

Date visited: .... Weather: ☀ ⛅ ☁ ⛅ 🌧 ⛈ ☁ 🌨 🌨

Traveling companions: ....

Where we stayed: ....

What we did: ....

....

....

Sights seen: ....

....

....

Wildlife seen: ....

....

....

Favorite moments: ....

....

....

....

....

....

....

....

....

PASSPORT STAMP(S)

Favorite attractions:

Visit again?   Park rating: ☆ ☆ ☆ ☆ ☆

Things to remember for next time:

NOTES

WEIR FARM
NATIONAL HISTORICAL PARK, CT

Date visited: .... Weather: ☀ ⛅ ☁ ⛅ 🌧 ⛈ ☁ 🌨 🌨

Traveling companions: ....

Where we stayed: ....

What we did: ....

....

....

Sights seen: ....

....

....

Wildlife seen: ....

....

....

Favorite moments: ....

....

....

....

....

....

....

....

....

PASSPORT STAMP(S)

Favorite attractions:

Visit again?   Park rating: ☆ ☆ ☆ ☆ ☆

Things to remember for next time:

NOTES

OTHER PASSPORT STAMPS & PHOTOS